FLASHCARD BOOKS

CLOTHING

ENGLISH

to

SPANISH

FLASHCARD BOOK

BLACK & WHITE EDITION

HOW TO USE:

- READ THE ENGLISH WORD ON THE FIRST PAGE.

- IF YOU KNOW THE TRANSLATION SAY IT OUT LOUD.

- TURN THE PAGE AND SEE IF YOU GOT IT RIGHT.

- IF YOU GUESSED CORRECTLY, WELL DONE!
IF NOT, TRY READING THE WORD USING THE PHONETIC PRONUNCIATION GUIDE.

- NOW TRY THE NEXT PAGE.
THE MORE YOU PRACTICE THE BETTER YOU WILL GET!

BOOKS IN THIS SERIES:
ANIMALS
NUMBERS SHAPES AND COLORS
HOUSEHOLD ITEMS
CLOTHES

ALSO AVAILABLE IN OTHER LANGUAGES INCLUDING:

FRENCH, GERMAN, SPANISH, ITALIAN,

RUSSIAN, CHINESE, JAPANESE AND MORE.

WWW.FLASHCARDEBOOKS.COM

Infant bodysuit

El body de bebé

Ehl BOH-dee deh-beh-BEH

Backpack

La mochila

Lah moh-CHEE-lah

Baseball Cap

La gorra de béisbol

Lah GOHR-rah-deh base-ball

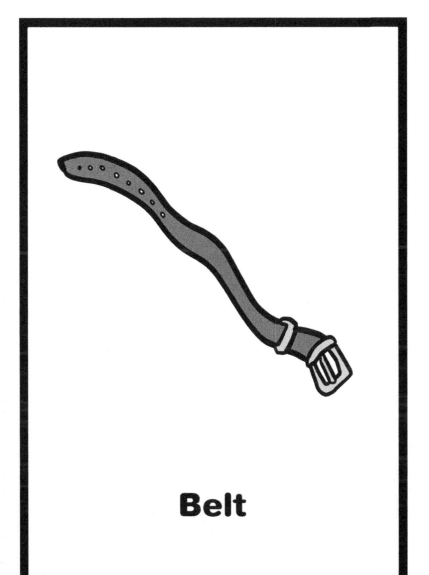

Belt

El cinturón

Ehl sihn-too-ROHN

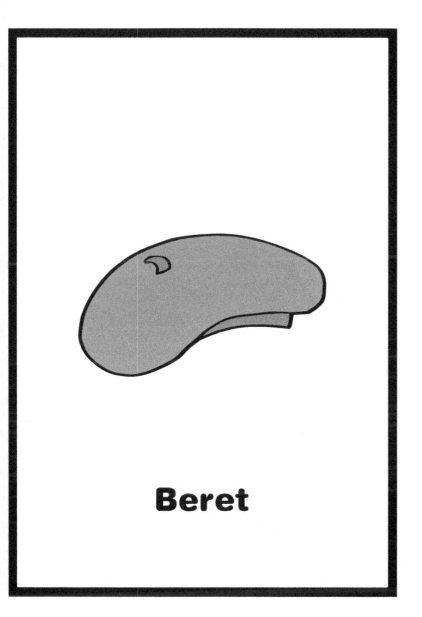

Beret

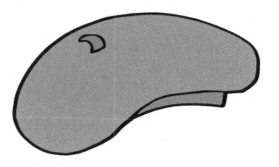

La boina

Lah BOH-EE-nah

Bib

El babero

Ehl bah-BEH-roh

Boots

Las botas

Lahs BOH-tahs

Bowtie

El corbatín

Ehl kohr-bah-TEEN

Boxer shorts

Los boxers

Lohs BOH-xers

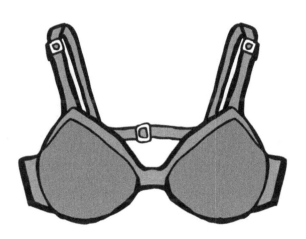

Bra

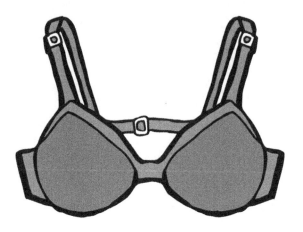

El sostén

Ehl sohs-TEHN

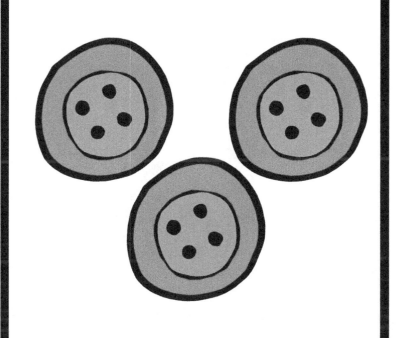

Buttons

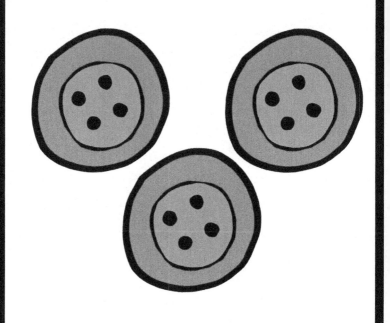

Los botones

Lohs boh-TOH-nehs

Cardigan

El cárdigan

Ehl KAHR-dee-gahn

Coat

El abrigo

Ehl ah-BREE-goh

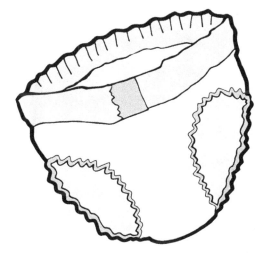

Diaper

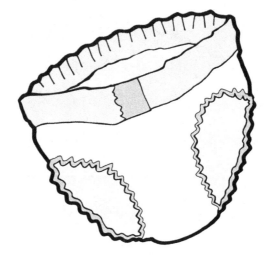

El pañal

Ehl pah-NYAHL

Dress

El vestido

Ehl vehs-TEE-doh

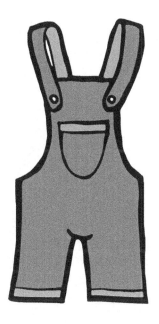

Dungarees

El overol

Ehl oh-vehr-ALL

Earrings

Los aros

Lohs AH-rohs

Glasses

Las gafas

Lahs GAH-phahs

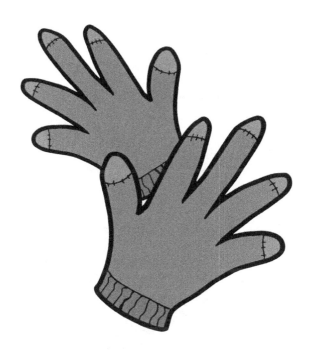

Gloves

Los guantes

Lohs GOO-AHN-tehs

Handbag

La bolsa

Lah BOHL-sah

Hoodie

La sudadera

Lah soo-dah-DEH-rah

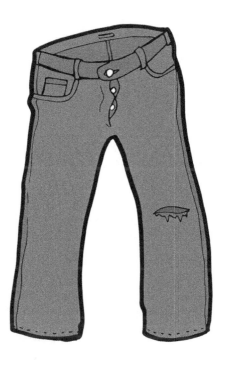

Jeans

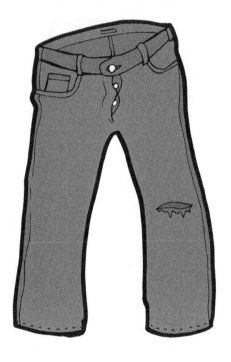

Los vaqueros

Lohs bah-KEH-rohs

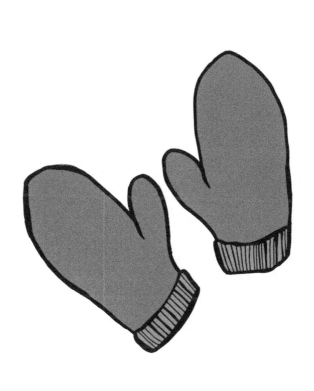

Mittens

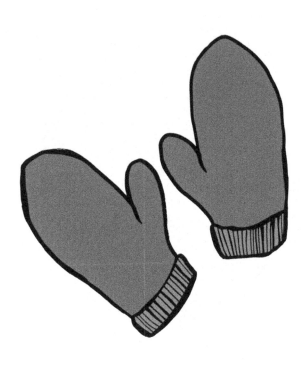

Los guantes

Lohs GOO-AHN-tehs

Necklace

El collar

Ehl koh-YAHR

Pajamas

la pijama

Lah PEE-ja-mah

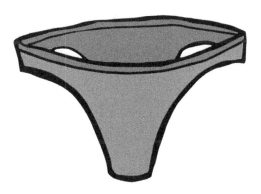

Panties

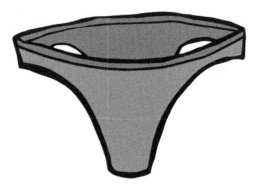

La bombacha

Lah bohm-BAH-chah

Party Hat

El sombrero de fiesta

Ehl sohm-BREH-roh deh fee-EHS-tah

Raincoat

El impermeable

Ehl eem-pehr-MEH-AH-bleh

Ring

El anillo

Ehl ah-NEE-yoh

Robe

La bata

Lah BAH-tah

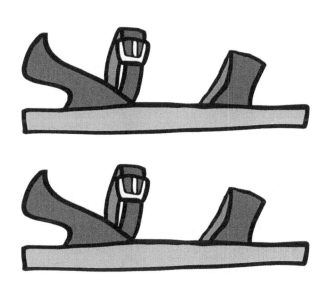

Sandals

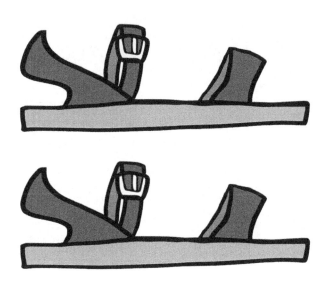

Las sandalias

Lahs sahn-DAH-lee-ahs

Scarf

La bufanda

Lah boo-PHAN-dah

Shirt

La camisa

Lah kah-MEE-sah

Shorts

Los shorts

Lohs SHORTS

Skirt

La falda

Lah FAHL-dah

Slippers

La pantuflas

Lahs pahn-TOO-phlahs

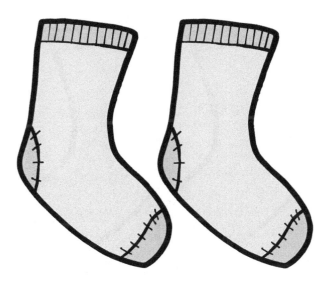

Socks

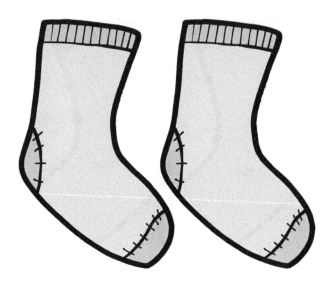

Los calcetines

Lohs kahl-seh-TEE-nehs

Suit

El traje

Ehl TRAH-heh

Sunglasses

Las gafas de sol

Lahs GAH-phahs-deh SOHL

Sweater

El suéter

Ehl SWEH-tehr

Bathing Suit

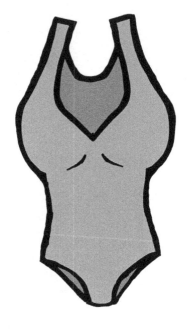

El traje de baño

Ehl TRAH-heh deh BAH-nyoh

Swimming Trunks

El bañador

Ehl bah-nyah-DOHR

T-shirt

La camiseta

Lah kah-mee-SEH-tah

Tie

La corbata

Lah kohr-BAH-tah

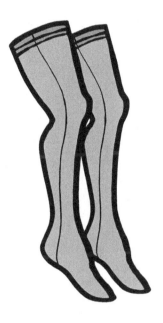

Tights

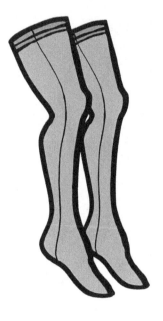

Las pantis

Lahs PAHN-ties

Top hat

La galera

Lah gah-LEH-rah

Sneakers

Las zapatillas

Lahs sah-pah-TEE-yahs

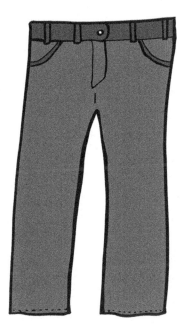

Trousers

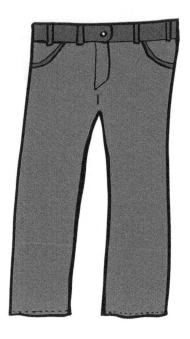

Los pantalones

Lohs pahn-tah-LOH-nehs

Umbrella

El paragüas

Ehl pah-RAH-goo-ahs

Underpants

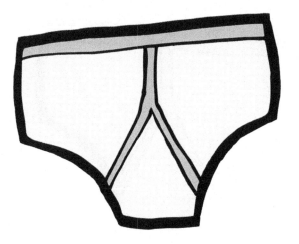

Los calzoncillos

Lohs KAHL-sohn-SIH-yohs

Vest

La camiseta

Lah kah-mee-SEH-tah

Waistcoat

El chaleco

Ehl chah-LEH-koh

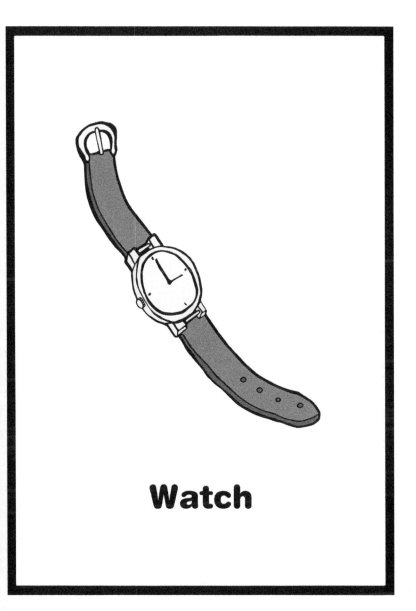

Watch

El reloj

Ehl reh-LOH

Rain boots

Las botas de lluvia

Lahs BOH-tahs-deh YOO-bee-ah

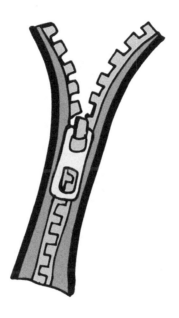

Zip

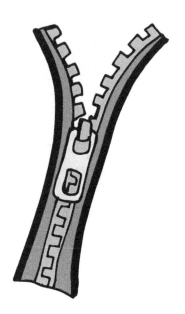

La cremallera

Lah kre-mah-YEH-rah

Made in the USA
Monee, IL
02 October 2021

79240042R00066